# LUGS
## BRANIGAN

AIDAN HARTE is a Kildare-based sculptor, best known for the *Púca of Clare* in 2022. He writes on culture for *Quillette*, *The Critic* and other publications. He is also the author of *The Wave Trilogy* (Hachette Books). He studied in the Florence Academy of Art. Before that, he directed *Skunk Fu*, the first TV show from the Oscar-nominated animation studio Cartoon Saloon.

SHEILA ARMSTRONG is a writer and editor from Sligo. She has worked on many children's books, including *The Great Irish Science Book*, *The Friendship Fairies* series, *Show Me The Science* and *The Great Big Irish Annual*. She lives in the Liberties and likes Irish history because it's a *stair* subject.

# LUGS
# BRANIGAN

The True Story of
**IRELAND'S
LEGENDARY
LAWMAN**

SHERIFF

e is the

WANTED
THE
ANIMAL GANGS

BOXI

MONDAY L

# Aidan Harte

with SHEILA ARMSTRONG

GILL BOOKS

Gill Books
Hume Avenue
Park West
Dublin 12
www.gillbooks.ie

Gill Books is an imprint of M.H. Gill and Co.

978 07171 89922

Designed by Bartek Janczak
Proofread by Jessica Spencer
Printed and bound in Sweden by Scandbook AB
This book is typeset in 12 on 23pt, IM FELL Great Primer.

The paper used in this book comes from the wood pulp of
sustainably managed forests.

A CIP catalogue record for this book is available from the
British Library.

5 4 3 2 1

To Dublin's latest and greatest criminal
mastermind, my niece Nicole Deegan

# Welcome to the Liberties

In the first years of the twentieth century, Dublin was a bustling place.

And no place was livelier than the Liberties, the oldest part of the city. It was called the Liberties because it used to be outside the city and was 'at liberty' to follow its own rules. Even when the city grew bigger and swallowed it up, the Liberties was still its own little world. There were people living there who had never been to

Grafton Street or St Stephen's Green – just a 15-minute walk away!

The Liberties was a busy neighbourhood, full of food and drink, crafts and trade. The air smelled like hops from the huge Guinness factory and, down at the docks, barges carrying barrels of beer chugged along the River Liffey. The narrow streets were packed with colourful carts selling fresh fish, fruit, flowers, meat, clothes, soap, coal and turf. The sellers called out loudly to every person walking by to show off their wares.

Electric trams and horse-drawn taxis rattled along, stuffed full of workers heading off to their shifts in the factories. The factories made everything you could think of: biscuits, bottles, clocks, coffins, sweets, shoes, matches, mattresses, umbrellas and uniforms.

2

The factory workers' jobs were dirty and dangerous, and the pay was terrible. They could easily be fired, and their families would be left with nothing. But trade unions fought to improve these awful conditions – members sang songs and marched in the streets for fair treatment.

## LOCKED OUT

A trade union is an organisation that supports workers' rights. Many employers did not like them because the unions wanted more money and fairer conditions. In 1913, employers decided to 'lock out' their workers if they joined a union. Eventually, without any money or food, the workers had to agree to leave their union and return to work. Even though they didn't win, the Dublin Lockout showed that the fight for better treatment was just beginning.

All across the Liberties, children played games like skipping, football and chasing, and they drew chalk pictures on the ground. The boys wore short trousers and the girls wore skirts or dresses. They were often barefoot because shoes were too expensive. Some of the children went to school, while others worked to help support their families.

Most people lived in **tenements,** which were large townhouses divided into flats. Lots of families lived together in each of these tenements – as many as one hundred people in one building! The chimneys were smoky, the windows were rattly and from some of the rooms you could look straight down through holes in the floor into the room below. There was no heating or proper furniture, and people often got sick. There was one shared toilet in the back garden, and the dirty waste flowed straight into the River Liffey.

Life in the tenements was hard, and the food wasn't much better. Breakfast was white bread and sugared tea. Dinner was potatoes, onions and cabbage, with a little bit of bacon or herring if you were lucky. There was no running water – buckets had to be carried up four or five flights of stairs, and then back down again with the dirty water. On their way up, the tenants kicked the doors to shoo away rats!

On the west side of the Liberties was a collection of buildings behind high stone walls. This was the **South Dublin Union**, a place where the poor and sick could go to get help. There was a workhouse, a hospital, a nursing home, a convent, a bakery, schools, playgrounds and houses for the people who worked at the Union.

John Branigan lived in one of these small houses with his new wife, Ellen. In the year 1910, Ellen would give birth to a baby boy they would call James Branigan, or Jim. They didn't know it at the time, but their son Jim would grow up to become Ireland's most famous Garda:

## The legendary
# LUGS BRANIGAN

# Little Lugs

John and Ellen Branigan lived a good life in the South Dublin Union. Jim's first few years were safe behind the walls of the Union, and he soon had brothers and a sister to play with.

In 1916, when Jim was six years old, the whole of Dublin came to a standstill. On Easter Monday, a group of Irish volunteers rebelled against the British government in Ireland. All over the city, men and women grabbed their guns and headed out to fight in the Easter Rising. They captured buildings and fighting broke out in shops, offices and even homes.

In the Liberties, there was hand-to-hand fighting, barricade-building and heavy gunfire. One volunteer even barged into the Branigans' home and fired out of the window! But slowly, the volunteers were beaten back, and forced to surrender.

One of the volunteers was a young man called **William T. Cosgrave**, a neighbour of the Branigans. Along with many others, he was captured by the British Army. As the soldiers marched the prisoners away, Ellen Branigan ran out from the crowd to shake her neighbour's hand. She had no fear! Cosgrave was a good friend to have – he would later become the leader of the **Irish Free State** when it was set up in 1922.

# LIBERTIES LILY

Lily Kempson lived with eleven other members of her family in a two-room tenement in the Liberties. She worked in the Jacob's Biscuit Factory but was fired after she joined a strike for fairer conditions. She was only 19 at the time of the Easter Rising but that didn't stop her. She fought at St Stephen's Green and acted as a messenger for the leader of the volunteers, Pádraic Pearse. She had to dodge bullets as she ran across the city, delivering messages. After the Rising, the police barged into her home, looking for her. Her grandmother sat up in bed and told them to get out. It was a good thing they did – because Lily had hidden guns under the old lady's mattress! Lily escaped to the United States and lived to be 99 years old – the longest-surviving volunteer.

As a child, Jim Branigan's favourite thing to do was to go to the cinema. The tickets cost fourpence and Jim would collect jam jars and do odd jobs to earn enough money to see the next movie. His favourites were **Westerns,** with cowboys, saloon bars, robberies and exciting shootouts with

outlaws. He liked the brave sheriff most of all – the guardian of the streets.

Primary school in Ireland was free, so all children could get an education. But some children from poor families had to leave school early. They helped their families sell things on the streets or looked after their brothers and sisters so their parents could go out to work. Jim was lucky – he stayed in school until the age of 14.

Afterwards, it was time for him to find a job. His friends went off to become factory workers, dockers, shoemakers, seamen and carpenters. Jim got a job as an apprentice with the **Great Southern Railways**, the company that was in charge of all the trains in Ireland. And Ireland had a lot of railway lines then – more than twice as many as it does now!

A job as a railway apprentice meant hard, dirty work helping fitters, boilermakers and metalworkers. Jim hated it. Even worse, the other railway workers didn't like him because he didn't come from an old railway family. They bullied him and beat him up – but he refused to fight back. He would come home from work with black eyes and a bloody nose, but he would go straight back the next day. He was shy and quiet, but he was **tough!**

# RAILWAY TIME

Did you know that Irish towns used to be on different times? Clocks in Cork were 11 minutes behind Dublin, while Belfast clocks were 1 minute and 19 seconds ahead. Imagine waiting for a train halfway between Cork and Belfast – what time would you need to be at the station? As trains became popular, the government passed a law to make sure that everyone was using the same time. But Dublin was still 25 minutes behind London. It was only in 1916 that Ireland changed to Greenwich Mean Time, which we still use today.

Jim was growing up into a tall and skinny teenager with thick sandy hair. One thing made him stand out among the other apprentices – his ears. They were massive and stuck out like two teacup handles from the side of his head. His big ears would give him a nickname that would follow him for the rest of his life:

## LUGS

# The New Recruit

A fter the Easter Rising, people were unhappy with how the leaders of the rebellion had been treated by the British Army. More and more people believed that Ireland should be in charge of itself and, eventually, the War of Independence broke out in 1919.

The main police force in Ireland at the time was the **Royal Irish Constabulary**. They were controlled by the British government and were very unpopular. During the War of Independence they would attack people and houses, set fires and kill civilians.

Meanwhile, Dublin had its own police force: the **Dublin Metropolitan Police.** They had a reputation for being harsh, especially towards poor people. During the Dublin Lockout, they ran at protesters with hard sticks called **batons** and broke up union meetings. They used to make people walk on their hands into the station while holding up their feet!

In 1921, the British and Irish governments signed a treaty to create the **Irish Free State.** This new state needed a new police force, but many people had bad memories of cruel treatment from the Royal Irish Constabulary and the Dublin Metropolitan Police. The Irish government wanted their new police force to be helpful and fair. They wanted officers to be trustworthy and an important part of the community. In 1924, that new force was given a name – **An Garda Síochána,** which means 'guardians of the peace'.

In 1929, Lugs Branigan was 19 years old. He was sick and tired of the work at the Great Southern Railways and decided it was time for a change. He was tall – six foot four inches – and everywhere he went, he stood out like a lamp post. His family thought Lugs would make a great Garda. Lugs thought so too – he quite fancied himself in a uniform!

## HEADY HEIGHTS

Six foot four doesn't seem especially tall nowadays. But a hundred years ago, the average Irish man was five foot five inches, and the average woman was just five foot tall, so Lugs was pretty exceptional. The reason people have gotten taller today has to do with health and nutrition. Pregnant women are healthier, and children get better food from a young age. Lugs must have seemed like a giant to those Dubliners!

But you couldn't just walk in and become a Garda. Lugs would need to apply and pass exams in Maths and Irish. He wasn't a great student, but with lots of study, he soon improved enough to pass the tests.

But there was one last problem: new Gardaí had to have a 42-inch chest, to make sure they were strong enough. That's about the length of a golf club wrapped in a circle – pretty big! But once Lugs had his mind set on something, he was **stubborn**. He trained hard for six months to build himself up, doing all sorts of exercises. When the time came to take the physical test, his chest had grown to 42 inches, and he passed – just about.

In June 1931, Lugs took the pledge and officially joined An Garda Síochána. It was **the proudest day of his life**.

Now he just needed some training, along with the other recruits. Life as a trainee Garda was tough. They had to learn all the rules and regulations of the new Irish State and different ways to keep the peace. They had to do exercise drills, hard work and lots of study – and the pay was only £2.50 a week!

## LAWFUL LADIES

The recruits were all men. Women weren't allowed into An Garda Síochána until 1959. Even then, women who were married were not allowed to work. This was called the marriage bar, and it meant that any woman who got married had to leave her job. It took until 1973 before women were allowed to keep their jobs – and their husbands!

Most of the other recruits were from the countryside and knew loads about farms. Poor Lugs thought that tomatoes grew underground, like potatoes. His new friends thought this was hilarious. But the country boys didn't know much about the big city. Lugs was born and bred in Dublin, so he was very comfortable among the busy streets and crowds of people.

By 1932, Lugs had passed his six months of Garda training. He dreaded getting a job posting anywhere but Dublin. He was a true Dub and hated the thought of the countryside! Thankfully, his first job was at the Garda Depot in Dublin, though he mostly found it boring. But that summer the Gardaí would face a huge challenge, and every new recruit would need to pitch in.

In June 1932, the 31st Eucharistic Congress took place in Dublin. This was a huge Catholic gathering that involved ceremonies, parades and public Masses. The Catholic Church was very powerful at this time, and the

Congress was one of the biggest events the city had ever seen. Dubliners decorated their homes and held celebrations in the streets. More than one million people came to the city, including visitors from all over the world. Seven ocean liners were moored in Dublin Port to act as floating hotels! Every Garda was called out to help control the crowds, including Lugs. And they were needed – a full quarter of the population of Ireland attended the final Mass in Phoenix Park!

Even though big events like this were exciting, Lugs's heart was back in the Liberties. He kept his head down and worked hard, learning from older Gardaí and getting experience on the streets of Dublin. Finally, in 1936, he asked for a transfer home – and got his wish.

Garda Branigan first hit the streets of the Liberties just before dawn. Lamplighters were putting out the street lamps before the sun came up. The milkman was doing his rounds in a horse and cart. Lugs stomped down the street and almost tripped over something ... it was a **dead body!** Some poor fellow had passed away during the night. But Lugs wasn't too fussed – he called for a doctor and continued on his rounds.

A few days later, he found himself in a much more difficult situation. On his early morning patrol, he came across a pregnant woman who had walked three miles trying to reach the Coombe Hospital. But it was too late: the baby was coming and there was only one person around to help. Lugs had to deliver a baby boy right there on the street!

Life and **death** were all part of a Garda's beat.

And Lugs loved every minute of it. His favourite thing to do was walk through the street markets, gossiping with the locals and listening to the music from the buskers and organ grinders. And everybody loved Lugs just as much as he loved them – they would tell him their news and sometimes pass on helpful tips about crimes.

Dublin City was filled with real characters.

**Johnny Forty-Coats** wore as many coats as possible, no matter the weather.

**Bang-Bang** would shoot people with his keys like he was in a Western, and people would pretend to shoot back.

Hairy Lemon was a dog catcher who got his name from his ginger hair and yellowy face.

Damn-the-Weather would sneak up behind people and roar 'damn the weather!' into their ears.

It wasn't all good fun – the city could be dangerous and often violent. But Lugs never once used his baton. Although that didn't mean he went easy on criminals – he had his fists instead. And he knew how to use them!

# Battling Branigan

**E**very Garda was expected to know how to fight. Back then, there was a boxing club on every street, so many new recruits already had some experience. Not Lugs though – he had spent years being beaten up by bullies every day but had never fought back. He had never even put on a pair of boxing gloves.

On his first day of training, he stepped into the ring for a practice fight.

His opponent wasn't much good either, but he managed to give Lugs a clattering. The same thing happened when they fought on the second day, and again on the third, fourth, fifth and sixth day. At this stage, Lugs had black eyes, bruised lips and a bleeding nose. **But he never gave up.** On the seventh day, he shut his eyes and swung at the other fighter. When he opened them again, the man was flat on the ground!

From then on, Lugs decided that he was going to train hard and become a great boxer. It was Lugs's dream to be good enough to box with the **Garda Boxing Club.** Skipping, weightlifting, shadow-boxing and sparring – all of these were part of his training routine, and he never seemed to get tired. Finally, he got his wish when he was invited to join the team. They spent hours train-ing together, fighting and improving their skills.

Lugs wasn't the most skilled boxer, but he had the heart of a champion. There are two ways to win a boxing match: knock your opponent out so they can't get up, or, if there is no knockout and the time has run out, the judges will decide the winner.

Lugs wasn't interested in knockouts. He was a big man, with big hands, and he didn't want to hurt people if he didn't have to. Instead, he loved the skill and technique of boxing. He never wanted to knock someone out – and his goal was to never be knocked out himself.

In 1936, after Lugs had been training for about five years, the Leinster boxing championships were being held in Portobello. Lugs was in the final. After three tough rounds, the two boxers waited to hear what the judges had decided. Finally, Lugs's arm was raised in the air. He was the new **Leinster heavyweight champion!** If only those railway bullies could have seen him that day.

27

After about five years with the Garda Boxing Club, Lugs was good enough to join them when they travelled around the world to fight. The Garda Boxing Club was full of real champions. They had travelled all over the world to fight and were part of the Irish team at the Olympic Games in 1928 and 1932.

In 1938, the Garda Boxing Club made a trip to Germany to fight in a big international tournament. Boxing was very popular around this time, and politicians as well as ordinary people watched each match carefully. World War I was over, but the next war was brewing, and countries were looking for ways to prove their strength.

# DOCTOR HERCULES

At the 1928 Olympics, Ireland's only winner was Pat O'Callaghan, a hammer-thrower from Cork. In 1932, Pat came back to try to win again, but the rules had changed. Instead of grass, the hammer throw would take place on a hard surface. But Pat had only brought spiked shoes that would get stuck! He found a hacksaw and cut off the spikes, returning just in time to throw the hammer and win gold again. Afterwards, Pat was offered the lead role of Tarzan in a Hollywood movie, but he came home to study medicine instead. He did try his hand at professional wrestling, though – his nickname was Doctor Hercules!

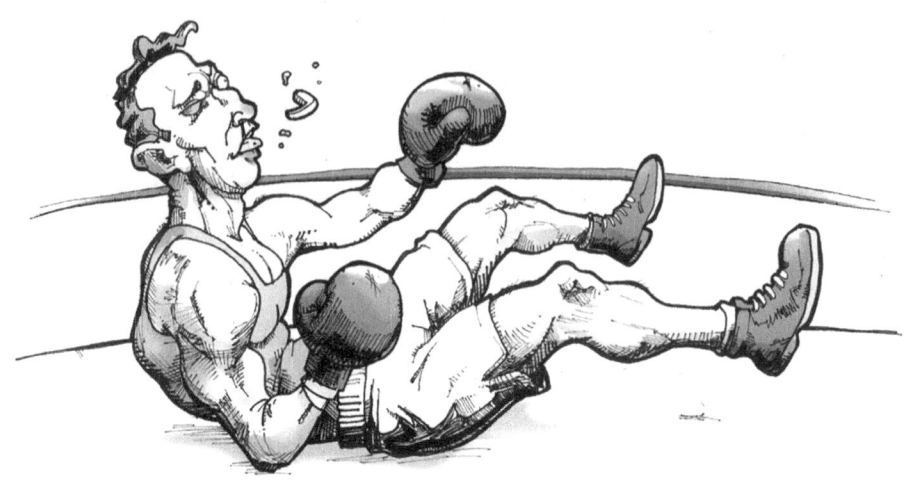

In Germany, the Gardaí were representing all of Ireland, which was still a very new state. They wanted to put on a good show in front of the bigger, stronger countries. Germany was led by Adolf Hitler and his dangerous Nazi party, who thought that their people were the best in the world. The Irish team would fight in front of a large crowd that included many of Hitler's top henchmen.

Lugs was up against a German who had a reputation for knocking people out. He was an aggressive fighter and would lash out with wicked punches to flatten his opponent. Lugs was knocked down three times in the first round. Three more times in the second round. And three more times in the third round. But each time, he got up – bruised, battered and exhausted – but he got up.

Finally, the match was over. Lugs had lost on points – but he hadn't been knocked out. The German crowd went wild, but not for the winner. Instead, they were cheering for the Irish policeman who kept standing back up.

Sadly, Lugs's boxing career was coming to an end. His doctor was worried that if Lugs kept taking punches like he had in Germany, he might get badly injured. He told Lugs that he should retire from the ring. Lugs was disappointed, but he followed the doctor's orders.

In all his years of boxing, he had never once been knocked out. This earned him another nickname that he would carry for the rest of his life: **Battling Branigan.**

# The Animal Gangs

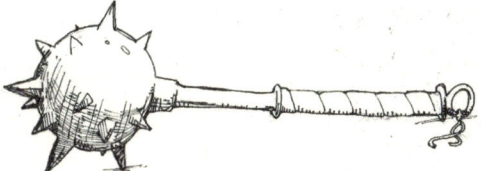

Dublin in the 1930s was a hard place to live. There were very few jobs and high levels of poverty. People were frustrated with politicians who weren't doing anything to help them. Often, young men hung around town because they had nothing else to do. They would join up with others and sometimes cause trouble by fighting and drinking too much.

They called themselves the **Animal Gangs**. They had names like The Tigers and The Hawk's Nest, or named themselves after the streets where they lived, like the

Ash Street Gang or the Stafford Street Gang. They loved to watch gangster movies and copied what they saw on screen – robberies, gambling and the gangster lifestyle. They were very snazzy dressers, with black shirts with white buttons, and flat caps with razor blades sewn into the brim.

The Animal Gangs would fight each other using all sorts of dangerous weapons. They would fight the Gardaí too, and the odds were always against the Gardaí. All of Dublin was afraid of these gangs.

But not Lugs.

If he saw a fight, Lugs would head over and walk into the middle of it. He knew if he showed that he was afraid, the Animals would have no respect for him. The best way to keep the gangs in line was to fight back. With years of boxing experience, his six-foot-four height and his massive hands, Lugs was the man to do it. He would fight them on the street and break apart the brawls. **Battling Branigan** was worth 10 policemen!

But the biggest challenge was yet to come at the **Battle of Baldoyle.**

Two bookies, one from the southside and one from the northside, were fighting over shady bets. They brought in the Animal Gangs to settle the score. Lugs could sense that something was up. He had a policeman's **instinct:** he knew the streets so well that he could feel when trouble was in the air.

On every corner there were mutters and sniggers, but the Animals were acting perfectly innocent. But the ladies of the Liberties knew everything that went on, and they trusted Lugs. He was born and bred in the Liberties, and as a Garda, he was becoming a very respected member of their little community. One whispered to him: 'There's going to be a fight at the races.'

Lugs reported back to his sergeant. Together, they found out that the Baldoyle races were happening that very day. They sent word to the other Gardaí to be on the lookout for troublemakers.

And it was a good thing they did.

It was a busy day at the races. People were showing off their best fashion and cheering for the horses as they raced around the track. Meanwhile, the two gangs from the northside and the southside were roaming the crowds. They were armed with knives, knuckle-dusters, pickaxes, tomahawks, cleavers, bars, bicycle chains, bayonets, hooks, hammers and swords – even

potatoes spiked with razor blades! And as soon as the Animals spotted each other, they were off – fists and weapons flying.

Because of Lugs's warning, the Gardaí were on high alert, and they raced over at the first signs of trouble. They managed to pull apart most of the fighters, but some escaped. Many were hurt, and a few were so badly injured that they nearly died. The leaders of it all, the two bookmakers, were far away – although one had parked his car on a nearby hill to watch the mayhem! At the end of the day, the Gardaí had to hire a truck to carry all the weapons away.

As the other Gardaí rounded up the fighters, Lugs was back on his home turf of the Liberties. He knew exactly who was behind this, but he needed proof. Off he went with his notebook, gathering evidence and asking questions, trying to figure out who the ringleaders were. Finally, he had enough proof to bring them to court, and the leaders were jailed. If not for Lugs's instinct that something was wrong, many more people could have been injured or even killed.

Two years later, at a football game, the Animal Gangs had a rematch. Just like before, Lugs began to pick up whispers of trouble. He had a feeling that a sports game would be a likely place for a rumble. Lugs checked the fixtures and saw that there was a soccer match due to happen at Tolka Park. This was it! He passed on his suspicions to the higher-ups.

Sure enough, on the day of the match, the Animals were on the prowl again. One gang found an unguarded turnstile and invaded Tolka Park stadium. The other came up the River Tolka on stolen rafts and climbed the walls to get in. They stabbed and punched and sliced and kicked at each other, screaming and howling as if they really were animals! There was chaos – the referee stopped the match and the crowd panicked.

After the battle, most of the Animals escaped alongside the innocent people leaving the sports ground. But Lugs wasn't having that – he knew exactly where to find them. He knew where everyone lived in the Liberties! A few days later he had them all rounded up and brought to court. This time, the judge came down hard on them, sending many of them to jail – and the Dublin gangsters finally listened.

Afterwards, one newspaper said: 'Garda Branigan will always be remembered in Dublin as the man who broke the Animal Gangs.'

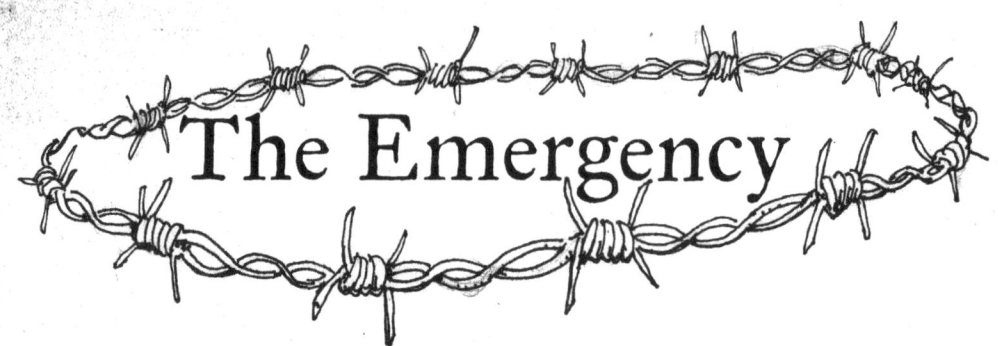

# The Emergency

B y 1940, trouble was brewing all over Europe. Just months before, Germany had invaded Poland. A few days after that, France and the United Kingdom declared war on Germany in return, and more and more countries had joined the fight. Soon, the battle lines were drawn.

The Allies were led by the United Kingdom, the United States of America and the Soviet Union.

The Axis was Germany, Italy and Japan.

In Ireland, World War II was called the Emergency. President Éamon De Valera thought that Ireland, which was a small and very new state, shouldn't get caught up in conflict between big countries. Most people agreed, so it was decided that Ireland would be neutral, which meant it didn't take either side.

Even though it was a neutral country, Ireland still felt the effects of the war. There were shortages of all sorts of things, like fuel, tea, cocoa, candles, sugar, soap, flour, tyres and tobacco. These goods were rationed carefully so that each household only got a certain amount. But black markets soon sprang up, where people would pay extra to get their hands on supplies. Some scoundrels would sell bags of tea that were mostly filled with sawdust! Lugs and the other Gardaí spent a lot of time cracking down on these black markets.

They also had to deal with **toss schools,** where people gambled over a coin game called pitch-and-toss. The game came over with the Vikings, so it was as old as Dublin City. The rules were simple: two half-pennies were put on a stick and tossed in the air. If they landed with two heads facing up, you won. Two harps meant you lost, and a head and a harp meant you tossed over again.

Toss schools were all fun and games until people began betting too much money. Gangs would get involved to collect debts, and deadly fights could break out over disagreements. Lugs and the Gardaí cracked down on the worst schools, but they could never stomp out pitch-and-toss entirely.

During the Emergency, there was also a **blackout.** This meant that everyone had to cover their lights at night-time, to hide from any warplanes that might be flying overhead. But sadly, that didn't always work. In May 1941, two German planes appeared in the Dublin night sky. They had gotten lost while on a bombing mission over the UK. The Irish Army shot up flares in the colours of the Irish flag to tell them that they were over neutral land, but the planes didn't turn around. Then the Army tried to fire at them, but the Germans dodged their missiles.

Just after midnight, the planes began to rain down bombs on Dublin City. The first fell on the North Circular Road, followed by another at Summerhill and a third in Phoenix Park, near Áras an Uachtaráin and Dublin Zoo. Nobody was killed, but the animals were quite upset!

The fourth bomb fell on the North Strand and did the most damage. The whole city shook as the bomb hit, destroying houses and shops, killing twenty-eight people and injuring hundreds.

Gardaí, ambulances and firefighters raced to the scene to help. All of Dublin was devasted by this horrible attack, but they were proud of the hard work that was done by the emergency services.

## HIDDEN MESSAGES

During the war, Ireland set up Coastal Watch stations to look out for fighter planes. Each station built a sign that could be seen from the sky – the letters E-I-R-E – to tell pilots that they were flying over neutral Ireland. These signs were twelve metres long and six metres high, and built of white stone. Many are overgrown and hidden now, but some have been restored. In 2018, a coastguard helicopter flying over Bray Head after a gorse fire spotted one in the middle of the burnt fields. It had been hidden for years. Locals fixed up the sign and repainted the letters.

Lugs Branigan did have one good thing in his life to distract him from the hardships of the Emergency. He had met a woman, **Elsie Armstrong,** who worked in a timber shop on Thomas Street. This was right in the middle of Lugs's beat, and soon he began visiting her regularly. They went to Phoenix Park, to dance halls and to the cinema to watch Westerns and musicals. In 1941, they were married by a priest called Father 'Flash' Kavanagh. He was legendary because he would 'flash' through Mass so he could get back to the pub!

The next year, Lugs and Elsie had a son, then later, a daughter and a second son. They bought a house on Drimnagh Road and began to make a home. Lugs was very happy there, looking after his children, his garden and his pets. He had two Alsatian dogs that protected his house and family. He was such a fan of Western films that he named them after two Native American heroes, Geronimo and Cochise. He had chickens and goats too, but his favourite pets were his **budgies**. His friends thought it was very strange to see Battling Branigan, with his massive hands, gently holding a tiny bird. He loved them so much that he even broke the law for them – he used to sneak budgies in from the UK in his pockets!

Meanwhile, the war continued across Europe. Ireland could only watch in horror as countries fell to the Axis, with tens of thousands killed or imprisoned. But the tide slowly began to turn, and the Allies soon gained the upper hand. In May 1945, the news broke that Germany had surrendered. When people heard the news, they ran out of their homes, offices and shops to celebrate.

The Emergency was over, and World War II was ending – but the smaller battles on the streets of Dublin would continue.

# The Sheriff in Town

Because of his experience with the Animal Gangs, and his hard work helping citizens during the Emergency, Lugs got a promotion. His new job was to deal with **street nuisances**. Now, a street nuisance could be any kind of troublemaker. Lugs could use his own judgement – he knew the difference between a messer and a real criminal. He had lots of names for the worst of them: gougers, bowsies, rowdies, ruffians, black-guards, hooligans and hardchaws.

This promotion meant that Lugs would be leaving the Liberties, but the whole of Dublin was now his beat. And it was tough work – Dublin was a rough city, so the streets could be dangerous. But no other Garda loved their job as much as Lugs. He always made the first arrest of the year, even if it meant driving around for hours on New Year's Eve, waiting for the stroke of midnight. This wasn't very fair to the poor citizens who were just celebrating the new year!

LUGS!

Lugs liked to think of himself as a sheriff from one of his Western movies, patrolling the streets and looking for outlaws. Everyone knew to be on their best behaviour when Lugs was on duty. When trouble broke out, he was first on the scene. Sometimes even the news that he was on his way was enough to calm a fight. 'Lugs is here!' someone would call out, and the troublemakers would slip away.

All Gardaí were armed with batons, but Lugs never used his. Even though he didn't fight in the ring anymore, he had kept up his boxing training and often refereed matches. But his fists weren't his most useful weapon.

Instead, he used a pair of **black gloves**. He didn't wear them – he held them rolled up in his hands. When he arrived at a fight, he would flick the gloves across the face of the troublemaker. This wouldn't hurt too much but it would shock the person into calming down. The flick of the gloves would often be enough to cool down the situation. Even the sight of those gloves could do the job!

Sometimes, though, the gloves weren't doing the trick, and Battling Branigan needed to bring out his fists for some **street justice**. If there was a fight going on, he would wade into the middle, pick out the ringleaders and hit them a whack.

A **clip** was a jab to calm a gouger down or stop them from hurting someone else.

A **clout** was stronger, for a dangerous hardchaw who wanted to fight.

A **clattering** was worst of all, but Lugs only doled this out to really vicious bullies and men who beat their wives.

Some people thought that Lugs played too rough. They thought he was a **bully**, using his strength and boxing skills against people who were weaker than him. And he didn't always follow the rules of An Garda Síochána himself. Instead of properly arresting people, he would often arrive on the scene, take off his coat and offer a bowsie a choice – to fight him or be locked up!

Lugs loved to go to court and tell the judge all about life on the streets. One time, he was arresting a hooligan who fought back, and even bit Lugs on the bum! Lugs told the judge he couldn't show him the wound – because he was sitting on it.

Even though Lugs could put the fear into the toughest gouger, there was a softer side to him too. Often, he would tell the judge that a person deserved a second chance. He didn't want people to be punished when they could learn a lesson instead. But if Lugs caught them at the same thing again, there would be no mercy!

He also looked after the **characters** of the city, like Johnny Forty-Coats, Bang-Bang and Damn-the-Weather. They often suffered from addiction, mental health problems or were dealing with injuries from fighting in the World Wars. Sometimes they would end up in court over some small trouble, but Lugs would be by their side, helping them through it.

Nobody loved Lugs better than the **women of Dublin.** Their lives were very hard – they had to look after their families on very little money, and many of them had husbands who would beat them black and blue. And if Lugs heard they were being mistreated, off he went after the culprit with his two fists, ready to teach him a lesson.

## UP TO MONTO

Many unfortunate girls had to work on the streets to earn money. They lived very difficult lives in places like Monto – a dirty, dangerous area in the north-east of Dublin. Monto was named after Montgomery Street, which was originally called World's End Lane. This was a fitting name because many of the women in Monto had nowhere else in the world to go. Their families had abandoned them, the Church was no help and most Gardaí would ignore them or treat them badly. But Lugs was different – he would always stop for a chat to see how they were doing. He tried to look out for them and protect them as best as he could.

All over Dublin – from the Liberties to the Liffey, Baldoyle to Ballybough, Mountjoy to Monto – people

were talking about Lugs
Branigan. To some people,
he was a **bully**, and to
others, he was a guard-
ian. But whether you
loved him or hated him,
there was no denying that
you knew his name.

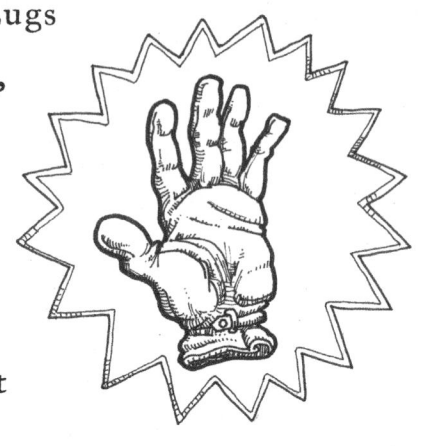

But he *hated* the nickname Lugs – if he ever heard
you call him that to his face, you were in for it. On the
streets, it was **Garda Branigan** – or you'd feel the flick
of his gloves!

# The Rock and Roll Cop

In 1950s Dublin, there was a new menace on the streets. It was maybe the toughest challenge Lugs had faced so far: **teenagers!**

Did you know that the whole idea of a teenager is still quite new? Up until about eighty years ago, you went from being a child to being an adult, with nothing in between. As families became wealthier, children didn't have to work and could stay in school longer. They began to develop their own culture and listen to music, read books and watch films that their parents didn't approve of. Not much has changed!

At that time, rock and roll was king, and teenagers couldn't get enough of it. They began to meet up and go to clubs and cinemas together. They would turn their jukeboxes up to full volume and jive all night long. The jive was a new sort of dance where you slapped your thighs, wiggled your hips and waved your hands in the air to the beat of the music. The parents of Dublin, who were used to gentle waltzes, thought these rebellious teens were a disgrace!

## THE KING

Elvis Presley was the King of Rock and Roll. His speciality was his dance moves – Rubber Legs, the Hip Swivel, the Slide and the Pelvis. Teenagers had never seen anything like this before, and everywhere Elvis went, the crowds went mad. His dance moves were so controversial that when he appeared on TV, they would only show him from the waist up! Elvis had roots in Co. Wicklow, but he never played a concert in Ireland. Even Lugs Branigan couldn't have handled that!

Some teenage rock and roll fans called themselves **Teddy Boys** because they were inspired by the clothes worn around the time of King Edward VII. They wore long Edwardian-style jackets with bright shirts, narrow trousers and thin ties. They wore their hair long, slicked back to make the coolest hairstyle of the time –

the duck's arse! The Teddy Boys even had their own lingo – these hepcats would boogie-woogie until twelve chimes, daddy-o!

Most of the Teddy Boys were just having fun and expressing them-selves, but some of them began to act out and cause trouble. They would carry flick knives, start fights with each other and would sometimes attack innocent people. They hated the police and threw insults and stones at them. Lugs Branigan wasn't having any of that! Often, it would only take one look at his famous **black gloves**, and the Teddy Boys would back down.

The Teddy Boys loved American movies – *Blackboard Jungle*, *Rebel Without a Cause* and *Rock Around the Clock* were some of their favourites. They would go to see them 10 or 20 times and would go wild at the best parts – dancing in the aisles, ripping out chairs and jiving like mad.

Lugs did not approve!

The cinema managers asked him to come in and keep order. He would stand at the back of the cinema, holding his black gloves, and the teenagers would be on their best behaviour. Although Lugs loved the cinema, these types of movies weren't his cup of tea – by the end, he had seen *Rock Around the Clock* a hundred times.

Worse still was when the band that starred in *Rock Around the Clock* came to Dublin. The teenagers were so excited they **rioted!**

When big stars like this came to town, they needed to be looked after, in case the fans got too rowdy. Of course, there was only one man for the job – Battling Branigan. Lugs acted as **bodyguard** for many visiting celebrities, like the singer Cliff Richard. Lugs was very impressed with Cliff because after his concert he made sure to ring his mum. Lugs was also delighted to look after star footballer George Best because he was a huge Manchester United fan.

A few years later, the Gardaí were preparing for a huge event: **Operation Beatles**. The Beatles – John, Paul, George and Ringo – were the biggest band in the world, and they drove their fans wild. Three thousand people had tickets to their show, but many more didn't and were waiting outside the theatre, hoping for a glimpse of the Fab Four. It didn't take long for the excitement to spill over – cars were overturned, windows smashed and one Garda even had a bin emptied over his head! Lugs was right in the middle of it all, but even his black gloves weren't enough to stop the mayhem that time.

In 1963, the news came down that a Hollywood film was going to be made in the Liberties. The star would be Richard Burton, and his wife was the most famous woman in Hollywood, **Elizabeth Taylor**. Somebody would need to look out for this golden couple, and Lugs was the man for the job. Elizabeth Taylor was shocked that the Irish fans were so polite. But really, they were only well-behaved because Lugs was by her side – all he had to do was tell them to go away, and off they went!

When she left Dublin, Elizabeth Taylor gave Lugs a signed autograph – '*Jimmy, you are the greatest!*'

# Branno 5 and Black Maria

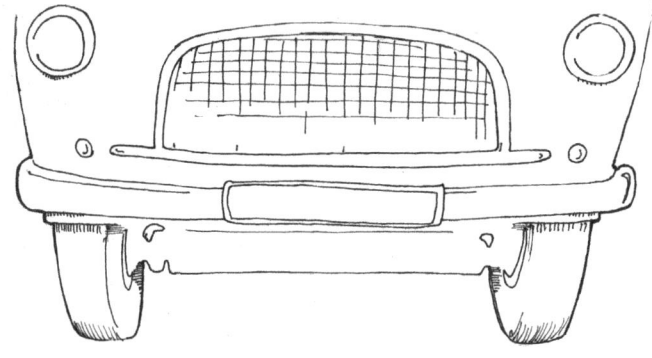

I n 1963, Lugs was promoted to sergeant. Most people were delighted, as he was by now a real Dublin hero. Someone even wrote a song about him and printed it in the newspaper.

Soon after the Civic Guards began

There joined a man named Branigan

He was a boxer, sound and grim

They called him Jim, Jim Branigan

But he still put them on the mat

He kept the peace both clean and trim

And he was Jim, Jim Branigan.

And now he is promoted up

To cause concern to many a pup

May more success come to him

Whom they call Jim, Jim Branigan!

Despite the best efforts of Sergeant Branigan, the streets of Dublin weren't getting any safer. He was only one man against an entire city. And crime was becoming a bigger problem – there were stabbings, assaults and burglaries almost every night. People complained that the city had become like a **jungle**, with dangerous animals on the prowl.

Lugs had a great idea for keeping order on the street: a **riot squad**. This would be a team of Gardaí that would drive around the city to wherever trouble was hottest. They could hop out and break up fights, then zoom off to the next hotspot.

He began recruiting a crack team of the best of the best. He wanted people who were strong fighters, brave, disciplined, loyal and fair. He didn't want any hotheads, show-offs or bullies. He wanted men just like himself.

To get around, they had a black van that would hold about eight people. Lugs always sat in the front seat, next to the driver, where he could see everything. The van even had a nickname – **Black Maria**.

Ordinary citizens smiled when they saw Black Maria trundling by, knowing that the area was under the watchful eye of Sergeant Branigan and his team. Troublemakers thought the opposite – knowing that Black Maria could quickly appear on the scene kept their hands in their pockets!

The van had a two-way radio, which was very high-tech for the time. The Garda HQ could call in a crime, and as quick as a flash, Black Maria was off. The van even had its own callsign: Bravo 5. But very soon, the radio would light up instead with: 'Come in, Branno 5!'

Jim Branigan much preferred the nickname **Branno** to Lugs!

Sundays to Thursdays were quiet nights, but the weekends in Dublin were like a **battleground**. Gangs would square up against each other. When Black Maria appeared, the shout would go up: 'Lugs is here!' The older fighters would disappear, but the younger ones, who hadn't heard about the power of Lugs's fists, would hang around. They soon learned!

Lots of people would also drink too much and start fights. For the first time, Lugs was having to deal with drunken women and was finding them just as tricky as the men!

70

## A LADY'S DRINK

In the past, women weren't allowed to drink in pubs. In many places, there were signs that said: 'Men Only'. In others, women could have a glass of wine or a brandy – but no pints. In the early 1970s, a group of 30 feminists went to a pub in Dublin. They ordered a round of brandies and a single pint, but the barman would only give them the brandy. The women simply drank their 30 brandies and walked out – without paying! Eventually, pub owners had to relax this rule and let women drink what they liked.

To keep the team's spirits up, Black Maria would stop by Drimnagh Road. There, Elsie Branigan would have a freshly baked apple tart ready for them to take on patrol. And they needed it because it was tough work.

But Lugs was a tough man – maybe **too tough**. Many people were afraid of him and didn't like the way he did things. He didn't always follow the law himself – he once told a man that if he ever saw him in the area again, he would shove a size 12 boot so far up his bum that his front teeth would jump out!

By this stage in his career, Lugs was over fifty years old. He had over thirty years of experience as a frontline Garda, but he wasn't slowing down anytime soon.

His next target was a bit different – **buses**. Gangs of young people were getting on buses and starting fights. Back then, there were only two workers on each bus: the driver, and the conductor who took the tickets. Conductors were being attacked regularly, and other passengers were afraid to get on certain buses.

Enter Lugs.

After some investigating, he figured out which routes were the most troublesome. Then, he and three other Gardaí would drive behind these buses in a plain car, ready to leap on board at the first sign of trouble. The gangs would never know if Lugs was close by, so they were on their best behaviour. But the bowsies soon caught on – they knew to look out for a tiny car with four **huge** men inside, their heads nearly touching the roof!

So Lugs came up with a different strategy. He would get on the bus, the same as any other passenger, and sit quietly on the top deck. A rowdy bunch would get on, screaming and shoving. But as they got to the top of the step and saw Lugs, leather gloves in his hands, they would go quiet. No other Garda would dare to do this – it could be twenty against one! – but his reputation was so legendary at this stage that even the sight of him was enough to stop crime.

Lugs Branigan had become a true legend of Dublin City. But there was one enemy Lugs couldn't fight. He was getting closer to the thing that frightened him most: retirement.

# Lugs's Last Stand

**W**ell into his sixties, Lugs Branigan kept up his sessions at the gym. He would lift weights and spar with men 40 years younger than him. He boasted that he could hardly feel their punches, that his arms and muscles were as thick as a crocodile's hide.

It was true that he had an incredible collection of battle scars. His shins were battered from kicks, his arms were pocked from knife slashes and he had even spent time in hospital for his injuries. At home, he had a collection of weapons that he had taken off street fighters:

knives, knuckledusters, iron bars, hatchets, picks, razors, chains, saws and swords. He would show them off to every visitor!

But fame came with downsides. In his 40 years as a Garda, Lugs had made enemies – and now that he was getting older, some of those criminals were out for revenge. And many young men wanted to prove their toughness by having a go at the legendary Lugs Branigan. Most of the time, he would spring back up and nab the offender, but other times, he could be badly hurt.

At 60 years old, he was the oldest Garda still on street patrol, and he was very proud of that. The whole of An Garda Síochána was proud of him too, so when he asked for a three-year extension before he retired, it was granted. He stayed on the street for three more years, fighting the good fight. But finally, he had to accept it – retirement was knocking on the door, and, in 1973, he had to let it in.

Lugs was devastated. Being a Garda was his whole world – he had spent most of his life in the uniform of An Garda Síochána. But Ireland was changing, and many people thought that older Gardaí like Lugs were **behind the times**. Clips, clouts and clatterings were becoming unpopular, and the government was bringing in new rules to protect citizens from unfair treatment.

# THE SOCIAL SEVENTIES

The 1970s in Ireland were a time of huge social change. Ireland first joined what would become the European Union in 1973, opening up opportunities for the whole country. The first computers began to appear, but it was only big organisations like banks and universities that could use them. Music exploded, and some of the biggest Irish bands began in this decade, like Thin Lizzy and U2. Women were demanding equal rights and equal pay. Meanwhile, up north, the Troubles were at their worst, with hundreds of people killed throughout the decade. The times were definitely a-changing!

On Lugs's last night with the Riot Squad, things were quiet. Everyone was very sad, and nobody knew what to say. Suddenly, a 999 emergency call came over the radio. The van raced off, but when they got to the location, it was all quiet. Everyone was puzzled. Then, women began to pop out from where they were hiding, laughing and cheering for Lugs. They were the ones who had made the fake 999 call! They gave him gifts and a card and took turns thanking him. He had been their protector on the streets, and now they had come to say goodbye.

Lugs found it hard to adjust to retired life. He took a job as a bouncer in a nightclub, keeping rowdies from the door. Who would argue with **Battling Branigan?**

He still took the bus into Dublin City and called into his old Garda station to give out advice to the younger Gardaí. They all respected him and listened carefully to his ideas. He would walk around the city, especially his beloved Liberties. And everyone was delighted to see him – they would tell him their news and he would give out advice. He couldn't walk down a street without being stopped by someone who wanted to share a story. Many said that he had helped them turn their lives around – a clout from Lugs was better than a criminal record.

Lugs's health began to get worse in his seventies. Not that he showed it – he hated being sick and would pretend to the doctors that he was just fine. Once, he did a handstand on a chair just to prove it! But he couldn't hide forever, and his doctors gave him the sad news that he had cancer. He spent some time in hospital, and he would tell every visitor that he would be getting out the following week. But it was not to be, and when he was 76 years old, he passed away.

Lugs Branigan's funeral was **massive**. There were all sorts of people there: Gardaí, politicians, journalists, judges, milkmen, street cleaners, shopkeepers, street workers – even gougers, bowsies and criminals. They had all come to say their final goodbye.

All of Dublin was **heartbroken** that day.

# Dublin's Watchman

Jim Branigan had many nicknames – Lugs, Battling Branigan, Branno. And he would be remembered as just as many things: a boxer, a bully, a terror, a gang-breaker, a bodyguard, a guardian.

His brand of street justice was tough, and in modern times, his behaviour would not be allowed. Even the worst criminals deserve fair treatment under the law. And Lugs didn't always get it right. Sometimes innocent people got caught up and injured by the Gardaí, and others were punished harshly for small crimes. Many teenagers, who were just trying to express themselves, were treated unfairly.

But times were **tough** – Ireland was a new country that had had to survive a World War and decades of poverty and violence. The streets needed to be tamed so ordinary citizens could live their lives. Criminals respected a hard man like Lugs, with his big fists and black gloves.

And Lugs could be **kind**, too. He often reached out a helping hand to a young person who got in trouble. He was a protector of the most vulnerable in society, at a time when many other people looked away.

He was many different things at the same time, because he was a real person – and real people are never perfectly good or perfectly bad.

Even today, stories are told about Lugs Branigan in the old parts of the city. In these stories, sometimes he is the hero, and sometimes he is the villain – and sometimes he is both.

Because one thing is for sure: the people of Dublin will never forget ...

The legend of Lugs Branigan.

# Jim 'Lugs' Branigan 1910–1986

1910    Jim is born in the Liberties on 6 January.

1913    The Dublin Lockout.

1914    World War I begins.

1916    *The Easter Rising ends with the execution of sixteen of the Rising's leaders.*

1918    World War I ends.

1919    *The Irish War of Independence begins.*

1921    *The Irish-Anglo Treaty is signed and the War of Independence ends.*

| 1922 | *The Civic Guard, later renamed as An Garda Síochána, is formed.* |
| 1922 | *The formation of the Irish Free State.* |
| 1924 | Jim leaves school to join the Great Southern Railways Company. |
| 1928 | *Ireland competes at the Amsterdam Olympics. Pat O'Callaghan is Ireland's only winner.* |
| 1929 | *The Great Depression begins.* |
| 1931 | Jim joins the Guards. He is Garda number 8005. |
| 1932 | *The 31st Eucharistic Congress is held in Dublin.* |
| 1933 | **The European Union is created.** |
| 1934 | *The Animal gangs emerge.* |
| 1936 | Jim starts working as a Guard in the Liberties. He becomes the Leinster heavyweight boxing champion in the same year. |
| 1938 | Jim takes part in boxing matches in Germany. |
| 1939 | Jim retires from the boxing ring and becomes a referee. World War II begins, known as 'The Emergency' in Ireland. |

| | |
|---|---|
| 1940 | The 'Battle of Baldoyle' takes place. |
| 1941 | Jim marries his sweetheart, Elizabeth. |
| | **Dublin is bombed by two German aircraft.** |
| 1942 | The 'Battle of Tolka Park' takes place. |
| 1945 | **World War II ends.** |
| 1958 | Jim is promoted to Detective Garda. |
| 1959 | *Women are legally allowed to join An Garda Síochána.* |
| 1961 | **The Berlin Wall is constructed.** |
| 1963 | Detective Sergeant Branigan roams the city in Branno 5. The same year, he is assigned as the personal bodyguard for Richard Burton and Elizabeth Taylor while they are filming in the Liberties. |
| 1973 | Jim retires. **Ireland joins the European Union.** |
| 1986 | Jim heads for the last round-up on 22 May. |